Library of Congress Cataloging-in-Publication Data

Torregrossa, Richard.
    Fun facts about cats: inspiring tales, amazing feats and helpful
hints / written and illustrated by Richard Torregrossa.
        p.   cm.
    Includes bibliographical references (p.   ).
    1. Cats—Miscellaneous.   I. Title.
SF445.5.T67   1998   98–6966
636.8—dc21   CIP

ISBN 1-55874-612-9

Publisher: Health Communications, Inc.
            3201 S.W. 15th Street
            Deerfield Beach, FL 33442-8190

Cover illustration by Richard Torregrossa
Cover design by Sandy Brandvold and Justine Wenman

'I love Fun Facts About Cats*! I train and care for
Morris, the 9-Lives cat, and this book is a stand-out
favorite in my collection. Richard Torregrossa skillfully
combines both education and fun facts about cats,
and with great affection—*Fun Facts About Cats *is
appropriately named. As someone who has spent over
a decade working with cats, I really appreciate this
book's combination of humane messages with a
healthy sense of humor."*

—**Dawn Haney**
handler, trainer, and spokesperson
for Morris, the 9-Lives Cat

FUN FACTS ABOUT CATS

Inspiring Tales, Amazing Feats and Helpful Hints

Written and Illustrated by

Richard Torregrossa

Health Communications, Inc.
Deerfield Beach, Florida

www.hci-online.com

This book is dedicated to
Judith Wilson.

Acknowledgments

I would like to thank my friends Ken and Justine Wenman for their help and encouragement; Carolyn Harmon, a cheerful and extremely competent researcher who zips around the World Wide Web like nobody else I know; and thanks to the pet-loving and hard-working people at Health Communications, Inc.— Peter Vegso, Christine Belleris and Allison "I'll Send it FedEx" Janse. Thanks to Lawna Oldfield and Sandy Brandvold for their creative and thoughtful graphic design.

Also, to Steven Kent, my literary and art agent, whose guiding light is always there—except when he's in London working with other clients.

Preface

I have a confession to make.

I don't own a cat. I haven't owned one in many many years. In fact, I'm deathly allergic to cats. Even to short hairs.

Why, then, am I writing and illustrating a book celebrating the very animal that makes my eyes itch, chest wheeze, and nose explode in an often uncontrollable series of windy sneezes?

Because I *love* cats. I really do. Always have. The havoc they inflict on my immune system has not dimmed my affection for them one bit. But unlike most of you cat lovers out there, I must worship them from afar—or after gulping down a handful of antihistamines.

I wasn't always allergic. As a kid, I had many cats, so I do have some first-hand experience with living, breathing felines. This book isn't a completely academic exercise.

Cats are cool. Cooler than any other animal I can think of. They are the James Dean of animals. The ones I had were playful, soft, mischievous, affectionate, wily, amusing, fascinating and deeply mysterious creatures that I sometimes still see in my dreams. I miss them, and that's why I've written this book. It's my way of keeping them in my life while avoiding "a reaction." So far so good.

I've created over one hundred pen-and-ink drawings of cats for this project and I haven't sneezed once. Not even a wheeze. This, then, might very well be the first hypoallergenic book.

And I've made the happy discovery that cats are as much fun to research and write about and draw as they are to handle on one's lap. Well, almost.

Nothing can replace the joy and love of having a warm, companionable cat at your side.

But should you have a sensitive nose like mine, you won't have to worry. And all of you cat lovers out there who aren't cursed with cat allergies can have twice the fun.

Richard Torregrossa
San Diego, California
April 1998

Cat Naps

Cats are nocturnal creatures, so they sleep about sixteen hours each day. Therefore, a seven-year-old cat has only been awake for about two years of its life.

The Pick of the Litter

When choosing a kitten look for the one that plays in the center of the litter. Research shows that this indicates good health and an amiable disposition.

Purr-fect Companions

Cats make such good house pets because they are willing to share affection when we are around and able to be self-sufficient when we're not. They're also superb listeners. One survey found that only 5 percent of all cat owners do not talk to their cats.

Cats and People

A study conducted by Temple University in the early 1980s found that when cats receive just a five-minute dose of attention of each day during early domestic life, they will become more attached to people.

Cats with Heart

A cat's heart beats twice as fast as a human heart—
110 to 140 beats per minute. The reason is, the smaller
the animal, the higher the heart rate. Small animals
also generally have a higher metabolic rate.

A Cat Tale

According to Russian folk wisdom, a person who brings home a cat should throw it immediately onto the bed. If the cat settles down promptly, it means the cat will stay with its new owner.

Black Cats

In the Middle Ages, cats were hunted and cursed as the devil incarnate.

Chow Time

According to experts, cats prefer the same food at the same time of day. The American Humane Society discourages feeding table scraps to pets, especially fatty and spicy foods. Some foods can even be deadly. Chocolate, for instance, contains the alkaloid theo-bromine, which is toxic to cats.

Groovy Grooming

To prevent their cat from having a bad hair day, 25 percent of pet owners blow dry their pet's hair after a bath.

See What I Mean?

Most cats can see six times better than people can in the dark.

Kitties and Mom

In the first two weeks of a kitten's life, its eyes are closed; the newborn finds its mother's milk through smell and touch.

Cool Cat

One reason why cats are so laid back and independent is that they are considered predators, not prey, in the animal world. Dogs are predators, too, but they prefer company—human or canine—if given the choice.

According to an article by Wendy Christensen in *Cat Fancy* magazine, "cats have independent spirits...." So the "cool cat" syndrome probably results more from temperament than any environmental factor.

Cats and Snacks

Experts recommend that cat treats should comprise no more than 5 percent of a cat's daily food intake.

Big Cat, Little Cat

The largest breed of cat is the Ragdoll. Males weigh between twelve and twenty pounds; females ten and fifteen pounds.

The smallest breed is the Singapura. Adult females weigh about four pounds and males about six pounds.

Persians are also small cats, usually weighing about six pounds, but they have so much hair they appear as if they weigh twice that amount.

If Your Cat Doesn't Come When You Call ...

... it may not be ignoring you: Many white cats with blue eyes are deaf. According to the Cat Fancier's Association, a white cat with two blue eyes has the highest chance of being deaf. If it has green or gold eyes, it has the lowest chance of being deaf. And if a cat has one blue eye and one green eye, its chances of being deaf fall somewhere in the middle.

Purebred white cats, however, are said to have a lower prevalence of deafness than mixed-breed white cats.

For Women Only

Wondering why even catnip and candlelight dinners can't get your calico cat in the mood for romance with Chlöe, the other calico on the block? Calico cats are always female, so you might try fixing her up with Rocky instead.

How Much Does
That Kitty *Really* Cost?

According to 1997 figures from the American Veterinary Medical Association, vet bills for cat owners average about eighty dollars per year for the life of their kitty.

Gesundheit!

An old Italian superstition says that a cat sneezing is a good omen for anyone who hears it.

Cat Scratch Fever

Cats don't scratch your furniture to annoy you or purposely ruin that armoire that's been in the family since 1943, but to sharpen their claws. Cats have scent glands in their paws that mark territory and warn other cats that "This is my turf, so stay clear."

Is That
Call for Kitty?

When you're talking on the telephone, does your cat suddenly become playful? Does it rub up against your leg? Swipe at the telephone cord?

The reason many cats try to interfere with their owner's telephone conversation is that kitty thinks you're talking to her, so she responds in an appropriately friendly way. Cats have no understanding that there is someone on the other end of the line.

How Much Do
You Love Your Cat?

Probably a lot, right? But the ancient Egyptians were really crazy about cats. They worshiped them as gods, literally, and anyone caught hunting or mistreating them in any way was put to death.

Many cat lovers take their pets everywhere, but the ancient Egyptians took it one step farther. They hoped to take their pets with them after death.

Prince Tuthmosis of Cairo, for instance, was buried with his cat, Mit. Provisions for the long journey into the afterlife were left for him and his Mit.

Names of pets were found inscribed on ancient Egyptian tombs. According to Dennis Doxey of the Egyptian section at the University of Pennsylvania's museum, this shows that their owners wanted to help bring the animals into the afterlife with them.

8 MUMMIED CAT 27348
EGYPT EXPLORATION [Abydos]

Show Time

The first cat show in the United States was held at New York City's Madison Square Garden in May 1895.

Cats Make History

On June 19, 1997, Andrew Lloyd Webber's *Cats* became the longest-running Broadway musical of all time.

In fifteen years, 2,706 pounds of yak hair have been used to make those fluffy cat costumes for the 231 actors who have appeared in the New York production.

According to *USA Today,* the makeup shop has gone through 603 eyeliners, 12,240 creme sticks, 4,119 powder puffs and 225 gallons of makeup remover.

Odder still is that they've also used 48,451 condoms, for which they've created a special use—to keep sweat off their body mikes.

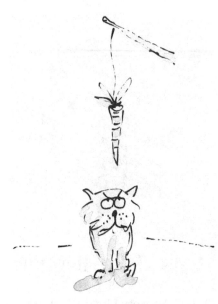

Veggie Cat

While the health benefits of a vegetarian diet for humans are well documented, for a cat there is nothing worse. Given a steady diet of veggies, a cat will become sick and eventually die a very miserable death. Cats are carnivores; they love meat and must have it to live healthy lives.

Super Cats

In Philadelphia a cat risked its own skin to save the lives of its young. Without the slightest hesitation, a mother cat rushed into a burning building and, one by one, pulled out her litter of kittens, incurring serious burns in the process. All of the kittens, however, were saved.

Stories like this one that relate the heroic efforts of mother cats are common. In 1996, a similar incident occurred in Brooklyn. Firefighters who responded to a report of a burning building discovered five tiny kittens purring outside the flame-engulfed building. Nearby was the mother cat, who had pulled them out one by one, according to witnesses. She finally collapsed with severe burns on her face and paws. She eventually recovered and offers of adoption and financial assistance poured in from as far away as Japan.

To Declaw or Not to Declaw

Is it cruel to have a cat declawed? Some people think so, for a number of reasons. Declawing a cat eliminates its natural means of self-defense. Second, claws are an important grooming tool; and third, they're used for hunting and climbing, which are essential for cats with an outdoor life. Other people think that indoor cats don't need claws since they don't hunt or use them for self-defense.

So if you're thinking about declawing your cat, think about whether Fluffy is an indoor or an outdoor feline.

Why Cats Seem to Like People Who Dislike Them

When a cat lover makes a noisy fuss over a pretty cat, the cat finds such behavior offensive, sometimes even threatening. It doesn't like loud, shrill sounds. The person who ignores the cat, however, wins it over because the cat interprets this as friendly behavior.

Clean Cats

Cats do not normally need baths because they clean themselves with their rough tongues; they spend about 30 percent of their waking hours grooming themselves.

Nevertheless, all cats benefit from regular grooming. Longhaired cats should be brushed once a day; shorthairs once a week. This helps keep their coats healthy and lustrous, and prevents them from swallowing too much fur when they wash. A bristle brush and a metal comb work best.

Eye Feel Sick

A possible sign of illness is when you can see your cat's nictitating membrane, or "third eyelid," at the corner of its eye. Other signs include refusal to eat, diarrhea, a messy coat, reclusive behavior and listlessness. If these symptoms appear for more than a day, take your cat to the vet.

Who's Smarter, Cats or Dogs?

Cats have long been given a bum rap in the intelligence department, at least when compared to dogs. One reason for this is that they don't train as easily. Another is that they don't score as high on "intelligence tests." But this is because dogs tend to think more like people. Cats are more complex.

Your cat can be trained just as effectively as a dog if you use the proper means of communication. So it may be the trainer's, not the cat's, intelligence that's at issue.

A Cure for Naughtiness

Hitting and spanking a cat aren't advisable—and usually not very effective because the cat will run away or fight back with angry force.

A better, more humane method is making loud, authoritative noises, either by clapping your hands or smacking a ruler against a magazine when your cat misbehaves. She'll interpret this as disapproval of her misdeed and likely be dissuaded from repeating it.

Is Your Cat a "Righty" or a "Lefty"?

Cats have right and left "hands," just like people. About 40 percent of cats are ambidextrous, another 40 percent are right-pawed and the rest are "lefties."

How and Why Do Cats Purr?

There are lots of theories; the most generally accepted is that the purring sound is caused by air turbulence created during the rapid contraction of the larynx and diaphragm muscles.

Cats purr for a variety of reasons. Purring begins in kittens at about one week old; it serves as a signal to the mother that the kittens are warm and not hungry.

Purring in adult cats might simply be a throwback to this earlier infantile behavior, indicating that the animal is relaxed and unlikely to attack, as well as warm and not hungry.

But deeper, more resonant purring in adult cats might be an expression of distress or physical pain. It's important, then, to know your cat's behavioral tendencies so that such an indication of pain or distress can be recognized and addressed.

Why Do Cats Eat Grass?

It used to be thought that cats ingested grass to induce vomiting when they were ill, but that's not exactly true. Many healthy cats enjoy a mouthful of grass now and then, so the reason they indulge in this habit is still a mystery.

It could be that they're trying to obtain a nutrient lacking in their diet. Or it could be for the same reason people chew gum—because they're bored and like the taste.

If your cat is a grass chewer, keep him away from lawns that are heavily fertilized. Chemical fertilizers can make cats sick. To avoid this, some cat owners grow their own grass indoors, in a planter or a flowerpot, and allow the cat to graze whenever it needs to.

Cats also like to chew on houseplants, some of which can make them ill. Plants toxic to cats include baby's breath, oleander, poinsettia, mistletoe and Easter lily. Although cats are generally careful about what they eat, it's a good idea to keep these plants out of their reach.

Successful Cats

Cats are one of the most successful groups of animals on earth. They thrive in more places than any other group of mammals.

The Largest Litter—Yikes!

The largest recorded number of kittens born in a lifetime of fertility to a single female cat is 420.

The Great Hunter

Although cats are very good hunters, they're not always successful at catching their prey. Birds are most elusive; they usually fly away before the cat can even get close to them. Cats have better luck with small animals, such as mice and cockroaches, but it still takes perhaps ten to twenty attempts before they catch one.

Unless you're Towser, the champion mouse catcher

who makes her home in a Scottish distillery. She is on record for having captured twenty-three thousand mice: the undisputed world's record.

Say What?

Unlike humans, cats don't have to move their heads to know what direction a sound is coming from. They just move their ears. A cat's hearing rates among the sharpest in the animal kingdom. She can hear your footsteps approaching from hundreds of feet away.

How Tabbies Got Their Name

Tabbies are among the world's oldest breed of cats; they appear in Egyptian tomb paintings from the Eighteenth and Nineteenth Dynasties, about 3,500 years ago.

But the word "tabby" seems to have been derived from a district in ancient Baghdad called Attabiah, where a special kind of silk was manufactured. The silk was known for its distinctive watered effect, which resembles the markings of modern tabbies.

How Many Cats Are There?

Today, there are more than 500 million domestic cats in the world, with 33 different breeds. The United States, home to more than 30 million cats, has 21 million households with cats living in them.

Who's the Friendliest Cat?

Siamese cats crave human company more than most other breeds, so they make very devoted pets. They are fastidiously clean, and are among the most entertaining and affectionate cats anywhere.

How Long Do Cats Live?

These days, cats are living longer—nearly twice as long as they did in 1930. On average, cats live fifteen to eighteen years, but some have lived more than thirty years. The oldest cat on record lived for thirty-six years and one day.

Cat Proverbs

*He that denies the cat skimmed
milk must give the mouse cream.*

A cat pent up becomes a lion.

Never put the kitty to watch your chickens.

The cat loves fish but
does not wish to wet its feet.

An Eye for Cats

Sight is the last of a cat's senses to develop. First is touch, then after about three days, the senses of smell and taste. A few days later the cat begins responding to sounds, and after about ten days its eyes begin to open. During this period, it is recommended that the cat be confined to a darkened place, until its eyes can fully adjust to light and shade.

Cat Tricks

While most people think of dogs as the perennial pet performers, cats can be trained just as well to perform many tricks including sit, stay, fetch, heel, and even play piano.

Cats with Cash

Some cats inherit astonishingly generous sums of money and real estate from their pet providers.

One cat in New York City inherited his own kitty condo. Cyrus, a seven-year-old cat, inherited a sumptuous $850,000 mansion in Bridgeport, Connecticut, that boasts a litter box in every one of its fifty rooms.

And in the early 1960s, two fifteen-year-old cats, Hellcat and Brownie, inherited nearly $500,000 from the estate of Dr. Willian Grier of San Diego.

Now, with this kind of good fortune, wouldn't you sleep better at night, even if you were a cat?

Colorful Cats

The color of a kitten's eyes changes as it grows older.

Cats with Bite

An adult cat has thirty-two teeth.

Mature Cats

Cats can become physically mature as early as three-and-a-half months old, but generally at eight to nine months.

Popular Cat Names

What's in a name? A lot according to cat owners. Fifty-one percent of them give their pets human names like Jake or Susie.

The most popular cat names today are Tiger and Samantha.

From Kitten to
Cat in Just Eight Weeks!

After eight weeks a kitten is ready to fend for itself
and can be safely removed from its mother.

Who Created the Cat?

It seems there is a myth for everything—even for the origin of cats.

According to Greek mythology, the moon goddess, Artemis, is believed to have created the cat in retaliation against her brother, Apollo, who created the lion to frighten her. As a kind of miniature lion, the cat was meant to ridicule him.

Survivalist Cats

Cats, as any cat fancier knows, are amazingly self-reliant and adaptable creatures. Although there are many stories testifying to this fact, there is one tale that stands out as particularly remarkable.

In Detroit, Michigan, a female cat was accidentally imprisoned inside a shipping crate full of motor parts. Six weeks later, in Egypt, the crate was opened.

Not only was the cat found alive, though pathetically weak, but she had given birth to a healthy litter of four kittens. The entire family had survived in complete darkness without food or water. Miraculously, the mother had fed her young and kept them alive during the long ordeal.

Pregnant Cats

The gestation period for kittens is usually about sixty-three days. The actual birth takes about two hours, varying according to the physical condition of the mother and the size of the litter.

Do Cats Really Have Nine Lives?

There is much evidence that they do. In fact, in England, a Siamese cat named Sam, survived an incredible series of near-death experiences, everything from hanging to being nearly done in by a garbage truck.

Dennis Bardens tells Sam's story in *Psychic Animals:*

Sam was dropped on the doorstep and sustained a cracked jaw. . . . He next disappeared while his owners were out visiting. His piteous mews at last located him behind a brand-new ornamental fireplace, which had to be ripped out to release him. Next he ate a bee, which stung him in revenge. His head became swollen and he could not eat for a fortnight. Next he slipped inside a laundry bag just in time to be tumbled into the washing machine where, fortunately for him, he was spotted. He then decided to join the rubbish being ground up in a passing garbage truck; the driver heard his 'plaintive mew' just before tipping the dustbin in. Next, Sam was found hanging by his collar from a tree. His eighth life was squandered when the home caught fire; he had passed out and a fireman revived him with the kiss of life!

There are many such cases on record testifying to the extraordinary survival skills of cats like Sam, and this is probably how the phrase "a cat has nine lives" got started centuries ago.

A Cat with a Record

Sam's exploits are pretty incredible, but Andy, whose owner was Florida Senator Ken Myer, has him beat by a mile. Well maybe not a mile, but sixteen stories at least.

In the 1970s, Andy survived a fall from the sixteenth floor of an apartment building. This gave him the dubious distinction of holding the world's record for a non-fatal feline free fall.

Do Cats Always Land on Their Feet?

Falling cats do not always land on their feet, but they do have an extraordinary ability to "parachute" to safety by spreading their legs and arching their backs. Some have survived falls of thirty-two stories.

A pregnant cat in Portland, Oregon, for instance, was accidentally knocked off a bridge. Not only did she survive, but she gave birth to a healthy litter of kittens days later. She also stole Andy's title of world champion feline free-faller.

Do Cats Smell
with Their Mouths?

Yes, they do. It's called the Flehmen reaction. The cat sucks in pheromones through the nasal cavity to an area of cells that specializes in processing them. This area is known as Jacobson's organ and lies in the roof of the cat's mouth.

Some Cats Go
to Great Lengths

There are many cases of cats trailing their owners over great distances. Scientists term this "psychical propensity-trailing."

Probably one of the most astonishing cases concerns Sugar, a cream-colored Persian, that trailed her owners approximately 1,500 miles across treacherous terrain.

The family was planning to move from California to Oklahoma, but on the day of the move the cat refused to go with them, probably because it was frightened by all the commotion. Sugar was taken in by neighbors but disappeared shortly thereafter.

No one heard from Sugar until fourteen months later. She had somehow managed to traverse the Great Plains and the Rocky Mountains to find her original family, now settled in Oklahoma.

And there was no mistake that it was Sugar and not some look-alike cat. A deformity of the cat's left hip joint proved beyond a doubt that this was indeed Sugar.

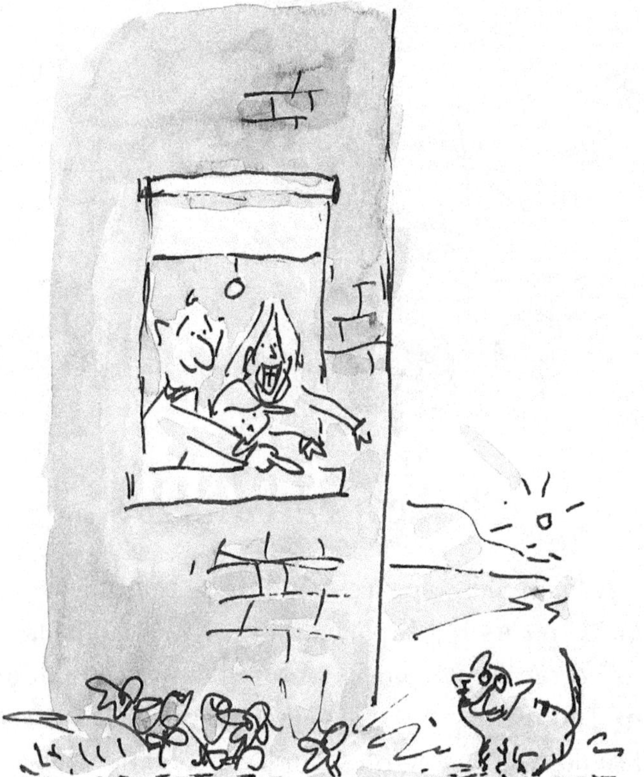

Shakespearean Cats

William Shakespeare made more than forty references to cats in his plays. Many of them appeared in his better-known works, but none were complimentary. For instance, in *All's Well That Ends Well,* he wrote: "I could endure anything but a cat. And now he's a cat to me. . . . A pox upon him! For he is more and more a cat."

And it gets worse. In *Much Ado About Nothing,* we find: "What though care killed a cat." And in *Cymbeline:* "Creatures vile as cats …".

What's the probable reason for this? At the time, cats were beginning to be associated with witchcraft and thus spurned by the population.

Cat Haters
Throughout History

Shakespeare, unfortunately, had good company among historical figures who disliked cats. President Dwight Eisenhower banished cats from the White House. In fact, he hated felines so intensely that he ordered his staff to shoot them on sight should they discover any roaming the grounds.

Johannes Brahms was another illustrious cat hater. Although he composed some of the most beautiful music ever written, his inspiration was certainly not derived from the company of felines. He refused to go near them.

But probably the historical figure with the most extreme response to cats was Napoleon Bonaparte. He suffered from a clinical cat phobia and was a true ailurophobe—the technical term for people who have an irrational fear of felines.

One evening, a member of his staff found him furiously waving his cutlass around his royal bedroom. The

emperor was trembling and sweating profusely—a basket case, in contemporary parlance. The reason? He thought a cat was hiding behind the window curtain. Apparently, all the profound courage he had displayed during many campaigns to conquer Europe left him when he faced a wandering kitty.

Experts say that the cause of ailurophobia probably stems from a childhood incident in which the sufferer was either frightened or attacked by a cat. But it is treatable. One therapeutic technique involves gradually relearning how to associate with cats.

Great Cat Lovers in History

Don't worry—there are far more famous cat lovers than cat haters on record. For instance, Abraham Lincoln loved cats. According to his biographer, William Herndon, whenever Honest Abe felt weary from the burdens of his office, he would "stop thought and get down and play with a little ... kitten to recover."

The Italian dictator Mussolini was also a renowned cat lover. He owned a splendid Persian cat for whom he cared deeply. In fact, he loved the cat so much that after it died, he had it stuffed so that it could continue to take breakfast with the family, as was its custom, and keep his young daughter company.

Surely, Brigitte Bardot must occupy a top spot on the list of famous folks who love cats. She founded the Bardot Foundation of Saint-Tropez, an organization dedicated to caring for animals—especially cats, for which Ms. Bardot has a special fondness. In her own home she accommodates sixty neutered stray cats, many of which are allowed to sleep with her at night.

A Great Writer and His Cats

The great author Ernest Hemingway was also a fanatical cat lover. Although this might not jive with his image as a macho hunter of big game, at heart, Papa Hemingway had a soft spot for felines. In fact, he wrote one of his most famous novels, *For Whom the Bell Tolls*, at a desk crawling with cats. The cat population at the Hemingway residence reached thirty-four at one time.

When he shot himself in 1961, Hemingway's home in Key West, Florida, was turned into a museum, where the descendants of those cats live to this day. Their offspring are quite prolific. In an effort to keep the cat population there manageable, some of Papa's "celebrity kitties" are periodically sold to the public.

The cats are unique not only because of their association with one of the greatest writers of the twentieth century, but also because some of them have extra toes, a breeding abnormality that has been passed on from one cat generation to the next.

Great Quotes About Cats

*Dogs come when they are called;
cats take a message and
get back to you.*

—MARY BLY

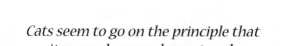

*Cats seem to go on the principle that
it never does any harm to ask
for what you want.*

—JOSEPH WOOD KRUTCH

Cats and Chemo

The University of Cincinnati Medical Center has started a special program to treat animals with cancer, many of them cats. According to an article by Cindy Starr in *The San Diego Union-Tribune*, the Veterinary Cancer Control Program there is providing radiation and other cancer treatments to animal patients similar to treatment provided to people.

Dr. David Denman, associate professor of radiation oncology and director of the center explained, "I'm not aware of any other medical school in the United States that has human machines just for veterinary patients."

One of the program's success stories is Thor, a nine-year-old Norwegian forest cat owned by Ed Dowling of Cincinnati. Thor underwent surgery for a tumor between the shoulder blades by his regular veterinarian, but was given only a fifty-fifty chance that the tumor would not return.

Those odds weren't good enough for Dowling, so he placed Thor in the Cancer Control Program for radiation treatment. Now Thor's chances of living cancer-free are greatly increased.

Thor might have survived without the radiation, but Dowling felt that, "Fifty-fifty is lousy odds. It's good if you're playing the lottery, but terrible if it's whether you live or die."

The Cat as a Role Model

"I think one reason we admire cats, those of us who do, is their proficiency in one-upmanship," said Barbara Webster. "They always seem to come out on top, no matter what they are doing—or pretend they do. Rarely do you see a cat discomfited. They have no conscience, and they never regret. Maybe we secretly envy them."

Great Cats in History

It might surprise you to know that Edgar Allan Poe, author of *The Black Cat*, a horrific tale of cat mutilation, was a cat lover. In fact his cat, Catterina, served a very special purpose in the Poe household. When Poe's wife, Virginia, was ill, the family was so poor they couldn't afford enough coal to keep the house warm. Blankets were also scarce, so Catterina would recline on Virginia's chest, giving her much-needed body heat. The cat was a kind of living blanket that helped keep Virginia warm and comfortable during her illness. In return, the cat received much tenderness and love from the Poe family.

Cat Hair Everywhere

Here's a handy tip for cleaning up all that shedded cat hair. Spray static remover spray on the hair-laden surface, wait one minute, then wipe up with a six-inch brush.

How Do Cats Get Their Stripes?

Darker hair at the extremities is known as "points." "With pointed cats," writes Kitty Angell in *Cats* magazine, "the amount of pigment in the hair depends on the temperature of the surrounding skin; the lower the temperature, the greater the amount of pigment produced.

"Therefore, the characteristic accumulation of pigment at the points is due to the skin temperature in those areas being a few degrees lower than the rest of the body."

Water-Loving Cats

Cats hate baths and water in general, although there is one notable exception. The Van cat, a breed native to Turkey and rarely seen in this country, loves to swim.

A Word or Two
About Cat Whiskers

The whiskers on your cat function as a kind of radar, and they are "the most sensitive of the sensory organs," according to the *Simon & Schuster Guide to Cats.* "They are situated in the skin above the lips and sense the slightest touch or pressure. In the dark of the night, when not even the eyes can find a ray of light, in a room or outside, the whiskers assume the function of radar that perceives the presence and nature of a nearby object. They also protect the cat's sight from every potentially dangerous object (a thornbush, wall, trap) that touches the whiskers first, so that the cat closes its eyes immediately."

Cutting or trimming a cat's whiskers, then, would be severely disabling to your pet.

The Divine Cat

Some Buddhists in Asia attribute divine powers to the cat. They believe that in the hereafter the soul of a cat speaks to the Buddha in favor of its owner who still lives on earth. They also believe that the faithful will return to earth in the form of a cat.

Cats and Cash

In an average year, cat owners in the United States spend $2.15 billion on cat food—and $295 million on kitty litter.

Why Cats Do That
Weird Thing with Their Backs

When it's cornered or threatened in any way, a cat will arch its back, and its fur will seem to stand on end. This makes the cat appear larger, and hopefully more formidable, to its opponent.

Cat Stops
Burglar in His Tracks

Guard dogs are common, but guard cats? That's a new concept, and one that seems to have been invented solely by a rather unique cat named Jake, who resides in San Diego, California.

According to *The San Diego Union-Tribune*, Jake was snoozing peacefully on the living-room couch at 2:22 A.M., when an intruder broke into the home of his owner, a woman in her early thirties. The intruder put his hand over the woman's mouth and told her not to make a sound.

That's when Jake leaped into action, scratching and clawing the intruder until he finally gave up and ran out of the house. Later, the man was apprehended by police and identified as the woman's neighbor. Detectives said that he had the telltale signs of a cat attack—scratches all over his arms and shoulders.

Jake's aggressiveness is all the more unusual when you consider his age: he's no youngster. In fact, in cat years he's ancient—over one hundred years old! (He's twenty-one in human years.) But he's still appreciated by his owner, who said, "When he was young, he was feisty. Now he has his moments."

A Cat Tail

A cat's tail not only expresses a cat's mood and disposition, it also helps the cat to maintain balance when jumping or falling. But cats, as you've probably already observed, get along quite well without them. Many alley cats lose their tails in accidents or fights but don't seem to be much affected by their loss.

Karate Cats

Sometimes your cat seems preternaturally intelligent, but no matter how smart you think your cat is, it can't learn karate. But it can teach it (not literally, of course).

The ancient Chinese, who admired the cat's quickness, agility and relaxed readiness in the face of danger or attack, developed a good deal of their system of martial arts based on the expert fighting techniques exhibited by the feline. In kung fu, kajukembo, kempo karate and other martial arts styles, many stances and strikes are named after the cat.

The "cat stance," for instance, is one of the first postures taught to beginning martial arts students. The object is to remain relaxed, yet alert and ready to spring forth and attack—like a cat.

The front leg of the martial artist is bent with the toes on the ground and the heel slightly off the ground. The majority of the weight is balanced on the rear leg; arms are raised and in the ready position; hands are shaped like claws, protecting the vital areas of the throat and heart. Once learned, it is such an effective technique that it is used by experts as well as beginners.

Cats That Blink

Blinking is a sure sign that your cat is in a peaceful, relaxed mood.

A Cat on Its Toes

Svelte and regal, the Siamese is surely one of the most beautiful breeds in the world, but it is prone to polydactylism—the technical term for having extra toes.

Yogic Cats

Spiritual masters, as well as deadly martial artists, have profited from studying the unique habits of the cat. Centuries ago, Eastern vedas, or wise men, observed that cats arch their back and stretch their limbs after a nap or a longer rest. They concluded that the reason for this was to banish the stiffness and sluggishness that sometimes result from long periods of inactivity. The cat pose thus was born, which is now a part of many yoga routines.

According to *The Sivananda Companion to Yoga,* you should kneel on all fours, "inhale and lift one leg straight up behind you, raising your head at the same time. Hold the pose, breathing normally, then exhale and lower the leg. Change legs."

If done correctly and consistently, it is said to refresh the mind and body by increasing circulation.

A Solution for Allergy Sufferers

Many cat lovers are prevented from owning or even associating with cats because they have an allergic reaction to them. One solution to this dilemma might be the acquisition of a sphynx cat, otherwise known as a naked cat. It is completely furless and therefore does not produce the allergens that cause such distress to people who are allergic to the fur found on most breeds of cats.

Queen of Pain

When a Ragdoll cat is touched or held, it will completely relax or go limp, looking very much like a rag doll. The myth that this breed is incapable of feeling pain is just a myth—it is as responsive to pain as any cat—but it does tend to be a tranquil creature, even in the midst of the most harrowing circumstances.

Kitties Don't Like Milk

Contrary to popular belief, kittens cannot digest cow's milk; it's too high in milk sugar. Sheep's milk, however, is more to their liking.

Cats and the Law

If you own a cat and it causes harm to another person, you are responsible, and a lawsuit can be brought against you. It is therefore wise to take out an insurance policy for all pets, especially those that are allowed to run free and possibly endanger drivers or pedestrians.

Cats are Love on 4 LEGS

Works Cited

Alderton, David. *Pockets Cats.* New York: Dorling Kindersley, 1995.

Bardens, Dennis. *Psychic Animals: A Fascinating Investigation of Paranormal Behavior.* New York: Barnes & Noble, 1987.

Gilbert, R. John. *Cats Cats Cats Cats Cats.* London: Paul Hamlyn, Ltd., 1961.

Karsh, Eileen. Temple University doctorate study of cat behavior.

Loxton, Howard. 1991. *Usborne Spotter's Guides to Cats.* Great Britain: Usborne Publishing, Ltd.

Malone, Bill. *The 125 Most Asked Questions About Cats (And the Answers).* New York: Bill Adler Books, 1992.

Meixler, Louis. "Pharaohs, Their Pets: Both Wound Up as Mummies." *San Francisco Examiner* (Associated Press), 1 June 1997: A13.

Morris, Desmond. *Catlore.* New York: Crown Publishers, 1987.

Siegal, Mordecia. 1997. *Simon & Schuster Guide to Cats.* New York: Simon & Schuster.

Smith A., Carin. *Why Does My Cat Do That!* Emmaus, Penn.: Rodale Press, 1994.

Starr, Cindy. "Human-Type Therapy Gives Pets with Cancer a Fighting Chance." *The San Diego Union-Tribune* (Scripps Howard News Service), 17 June 1997: E-3.

Steiger, Brad. *Cats Incredible!* New York: Plume, 1994.

The Sivananda Yoga Center. *The Sivananda Companion to Yoga.* New York: A Fireside Book, 1983.

Thornton, Kelly. "Meeting Jake a Catastrophe For Intruder." *The San Diego Union-Tribune.* 3 May 1997: E5.

Weiss, Pola. *Cats and Their Ways.* Geneve: Editions Minerva, 1974.

Wexo, Bonnett John. *Little Cats Zoo Books 2.* San Diego, Calif.: Wildlife Education, Ltd, 1986.

Van Housen, Caty. "Bonding with Kitty." *The San Diego Union-Tribune,* Aug. 1997: E5.

Resources for Cat Lovers

American Cat Association
8101 Katherine Ave.
Panorama City, CA 91402
818-781-5656

American Cat Fancier's Association
P.O. Box 203
Point Lookout, MO 65726
417-334-5430

Cat Fancier's Federation
9509 Montgomery Rd.
Cincinnati, OH 45242
937-787-9009

The International Cat Association (TICA)
P.O. Box 2684
Harlingen, TX 78551
956-428-8046

Internet Sites

www.petcare@interconnect. com.au

www. petnet.av/petrivia library.html

About the Author

Richard Torregrossa is a journalist and an artist who has freelanced for *Cosmopolitan, Self, Yoga Journal,* Microsoft's on-line magazine *Sidewalk,* and other national and regional publications.

He is the compiler and illustrator of *The Little Book of Wisdom,* also published by Health Communications, Inc., and recently illustrated *Daily Meditations for Women Who Love Too Much* by bestselling author Robin Norwood. He is also the author and illustrator of *Fun Facts About Babies.*

Born in Brooklyn, New York, he now lives in San Diego, California, where he is currently working on a series of illustrated children's books that have tie-ins to their own Web sites.

121

NOTES